CONTENTS

- Introduction, 5
- Chowders
    - Corn Chowder, 10
    - Fish Chowder, 11
    - Clam Chowder, 12
- Main Dishes
    - Tourtière (Pork Pie), 13
    - Double-Crust Vermont Chicken Pie, 14
    - New England Boiled Dinner, 16
    - Red Flannel Hash, 18
    - Fannie Daddies (Fried Clams), 19
    - Codfish Cakes, 20
    - Lobster Newburg, 22
- Vegetables
    - Maple Acorn Squash, 23
    - Baked Beans, 24
    - Corn Pudding, 26
- Breads and Muffins
    - Cranberry-Nut Muffins, 27

Anadama Bread, 28
Brown Bread, 30
Johnnycakes, 32

Pies

Maine Blueberry Pie, 33
Boston Cream Pie, 34
Maple Pumpkin Pie, 37

Desserts and Cookies

Indian Pudding, 39
Joe Froggers (Soft Molasses Cookies), 40
Maple Cutouts, 42
Cranberry-Apple Crisp, 43
Blueberry Grunt, 44

And Furthermore

No-Cook Cranberry Relish, 45
Mincemeat, 46
Hot Clam Appetizers, 48

NEW ENGLAND SAMPLER

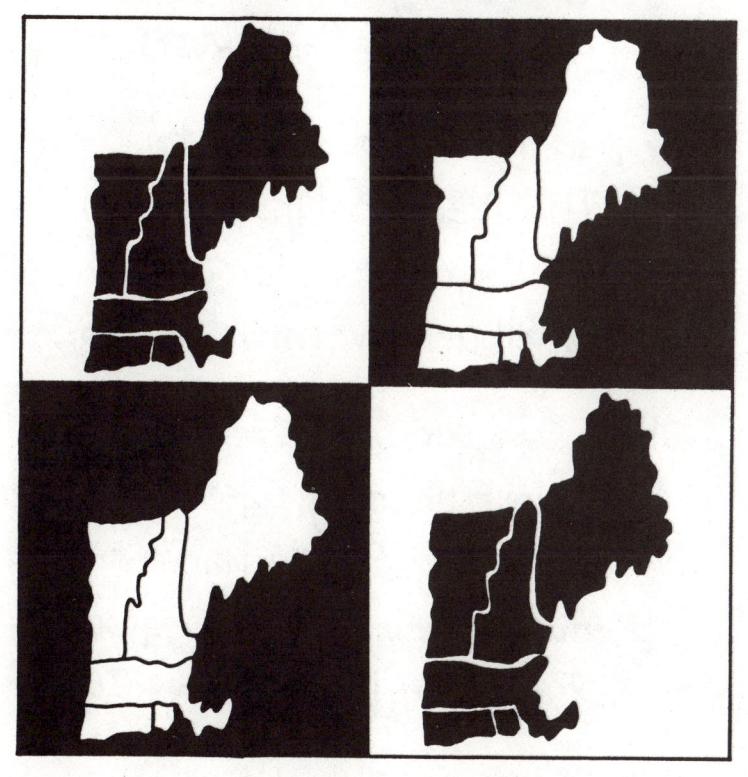

A Collection of
Traditional New England Recipes

by Jan Siegrist

THE NEW ENGLAND PRESS, INC.

© 1987 by Jan Siegrist
ALL RIGHTS RESERVED

For additional copies write to:
 The New England Press, Inc.
 P.O. Box 575
 Shelburne, Vermont 05482

Other Samplers available:
 Apple, Blueberry, Casserole, Cheese and Dairy, Cookie, Harvest, Holiday, Muffin, New England, Seafood, Strawberry, Whole Grain, Zucchini

Written and illustrated by
Jan Seygal Siegrist

ISBN 0-933050-48-8

PRINTED IN THE UNITED STATES OF AMERICA

INTRODUCTION

🫕 Mention New England cooking and what immediately comes to mind? Certainly, clam chowder, baked beans, Indian pudding, and the traditional Thanksgiving dinner with all its trimmings. But how about those less well-known dishes that reflect the New Englanders' thrifty nature—johnnycakes and New England boiled dinner? Or those dishes shaped by the early colonists' ethnic backgrounds—French Canadian tourtière and mincemeat? Then there are those dishes with outlandish names that originate in the colorful folklore of New England—Joe Froggers and Anadama bread. This book is a collection of familiar and not-so-familiar recipes—all are New England favorites.

🫕 New England cooking is shaped by a variety of influences—history and tradition, climate, and the availability of ingredients. The New England colonists had to adapt their cuisine to the new ingredients they found in

America. Most of the original New England cooking was based on three native crops: corn, squash, and beans. Corn was the number one crop. Whether used fresh, dried, or ground into cornmeal, this staple was used to create a variety of inexpensive and nutritious dishes from succotash and corn chowder to johnnycakes, brown bread, and Indian pudding.

- The New England colonists learned to prepare squash from the Indians. Pumpkins and winter squash varieties grew well in the harsh New England climate and were good keepers over the long, cold winters.

- Beans were another crop that thrived in New England's short growing season. Baked beans, a New England invention, was a result of Yankee practicality. The beans would cook slowly all day Saturday with the settlers' supply of bread for the week. Saturday evening they would be served hot with slices of brown bread. The leftover beans were then returned to the oven and kept warm for dinner after church on Sunday. Baked beans are still a favorite at New England church suppers.

- New England is famous for its fresh seafood. A variety of ocean fish, such as cod, haddock, and halibut, as well as such shellfish as clams, oysters, scallops, and lobsters, inhabit the rich fishing grounds along the Atlantic coast. Whether broiled, baked, fried, dried, or cooked in a chowder, seafood was and still is a mainstay in the New Englander's diet.

- While corn was king of the native crops, the lobster was and still is king of New England seafood, Maine being most famous for its lobsters. New Englanders prefer to boil their lobsters and eat them right out of the shells, although recipes abound for preparing this coastal delicacy.

- New England cooking minus seafood

basically describes the cuisine of Vermont. Beef, pork, chicken, and dairy products play a greater role in this land-locked state.

🍲 Cranberries are also important in New England cooking. The recumbent cranberry vines flourish in clean, damp beach sand along the New England coast. The Indians used to pound the cranberry with dried meat and melted animal fat to form pemmican, a long-keeping staple in their diet. Today, the tart berry is used to enliven pies, breads, salads, and relishes.

🍲 Another berry popular in New England, especially in Maine, is the blueberry. Early New England settlers used their primitive cooking equipment to create a dessert of stewed berries topped with dumplings. The sound the berries made as they cooked inspired the name "grunt." Later, when ovens were more common, the berries were baked in pies and muffins.

- Cheap, plentiful, and easily stored, the apple is a favorite New England ingredient. Apples are most frequently used for pies, often combined with cranberries or used as an ingredient in mincemeat.

- An overview of New England cooking would not be complete without mentioning maple syrup, a commonly used sweetener in many recipes. Pure maple syrup is used to enhance the flavor of breads, pies, cakes, cookies, and even baked beans.

- The recipes in this book are adaptations and modernized versions of a variety of New England favorites. All reflect the New Englanders' rich heritage and talent for good, creative cooking.

Corn Chowder

¼ pound salt pork, diced
2 medium-size onions, chopped
⅓ cup chopped celery
3 medium-size potatoes, cubed
2 cups water
½ teaspoon salt
⅛ teaspoon pepper
¼ teaspoon dried parsley
2 cups whole kernel corn
    or 1 (17-ounce) can corn, drained
2 cups milk
¼ cup all-purpose flour

In a large saucepan, fry the pork until almost crisp; add the onions and celery and sauté until lightly browned. Add the potatoes, 1½ cups of the water, salt, pepper, and parsley. Bring to a boil; reduce the heat and simmer until the potatoes are tender, about 15 minutes. Remove from the heat; stir in the corn and milk. Blend the flour with the remaining ½ cup water; stir into the chowder. Heat, stirring constantly, until thickened and piping hot; do not boil. Serves 4-6.

Fish Chowder

¼ pound salt pork, diced
2 pounds fish filets (haddock or cod)
3 medium-size potatoes, thinly sliced
1 large onion, thinly sliced
2 cups water
2 cups milk
1 teaspoon salt
½ teaspoon pepper

In a large saucepan, fry the pork until crisp; remove with a slotted spoon and reserve. Leave the drippings. Cut the fish filets into 1-inch cubes. Place half the fish in the saucepan; cover with half the potatoes, then half the onions. Repeat the layers. Add the water and cover the pan. Bring the mixture to a boil; reduce the heat and simmer until the potatoes are tender, about 15 minutes. Add the milk, salt, pepper and reserved pork. Slowly heat until piping hot; do not boil. Serves 4-6.

Clam Chowder

¼ pound salt pork, diced
1 medium-size onion, chopped
3 medium-size potatoes, cubed
3 cups water
2 dozen shucked hard-shell clams (cherrystone or littlenecks), chopped, with juices reserved or 2 (8-ounce) cans chopped clams
2 cups milk
½ cup light cream
½ teaspoon dried thyme
½ teaspoon salt
⅛ teaspoon pepper

In a large saucepan, fry the pork until almost crisp; add the onion and sauté until lightly browned. Add the potatoes and water. Bring to a boil; reduce the heat and simmer until the potatoes are tender, about 15 minutes. Stir in the chopped clams and their juices, the milk, cream, thyme, salt, and pepper. Heat almost to the boiling point. Serve immediately. Serves 4-6.

New Englanders insist real clam chowder includes milk or cream – never tomatoes.

Tourtière (Pork Pie)

1½ pounds ground pork
½ pound ground beef
¾ cup hot water
¼ teaspoon nutmeg
¼ teaspoon ground cloves
½ teaspoon cinnamon
1 teaspoon salt
½ teaspoon pepper
1 medium-size onion, chopped
1 cup bread crumbs
Pastry for a 10-inch, double-crust pie

In a large bowl, combine all of the ingredients except the pastry dough. Mix very well. Roll out half the pastry to form a bottom crust and place in a 10-inch pie pan. Fill with the meat mixture. Roll out the remaining pastry; place on top of the meat; press the edges together; trim. Flute the edges; cut slits in the top. Bake in a preheated 325°F oven for 1½ hours. Remove to a wire rack; cool 10 minutes before slicing. Serves 6.

Delicious served hot or cold.

Double-Crust Vermont Chicken Pie

4½-5-pound whole stewing chicken
1½ quarts water
1 large onion, quartered
4 carrots, cut in pieces
1 cup coarsely chopped celery
¼ teaspoon dried rosemary
½ teaspoon dried thyme
1½ teaspoons salt
1 teaspoon pepper
2 tablespoons butter or margarine
½ cup all-purpose flour
½ teaspoon salt
½ teaspoon pepper
Pastry for a 9-inch, double-crust pie

Place the chicken in a large pot; cover with the water. Add the onion, carrots, celery, rosemary, thyme, 1½ teaspoons salt, and 1 teaspoon pepper. Bring to a boil. Reduce the heat; cover and simmer until tender, about 1½ hours. Remove the chicken. Strain the broth and reserve. Remove the bones and skin from the chicken; discard. Cut the meat into 1-inch pieces.

🫕 Melt the butter or margarine in a large saucepan. Stir in the flour to make a smooth paste. Gradually add 2½ cups of the reserved broth. Cook over medium heat, stirring constantly, until the mixture is smooth and thickened. Add the remaining ½ teaspoon salt and ½ teaspoon pepper. Stir in the chicken.

🫕 Roll out half the pastry to form a bottom crust and place in a 9-inch deep pie pan. Pour in the chicken mixture. Roll out the remaining pastry; place on top of the chicken; press the edges together; trim. Flute the edges; cut slits in the top. Bake in a preheated 350°F. oven until browned, about 45 minutes. Remove to a wire rack; cool slightly before serving. Serves 6.

For variety, add a 10-ounce package of frozen peas to the filling before placing in the crust.

New England Boiled Dinner

4 pounds corned beef
6 medium-size beets
2 small parsnips, peeled and quartered
3 large carrots, peeled and quartered
1 large turnip, peeled and quartered
10 small white onions
6 medium-size potatoes, peeled and quartered
1 small head green cabbage, chopped
2 tablespoons chopped fresh parsley

Rinse the corned beef under running water to remove the surface brine. Place in a large pot and cover with cold water. Bring to a boil; skim off any scum that rises to the surface. Partially cover the pot; reduce the heat and simmer until tender, 4-6 hours. If necessary, add more hot water to keep the meat constantly covered. When done, remove the beef from the pot; cover with foil and keep warm. While the meat cooks, scrub the beets and cut off their tops. Place in a large saucepan and cover with cold water. Bring to a boil;

reduce the heat and simmer until tender, 30-60 minutes. Allow the beets to cool slightly; remove their skins. Return them to the pan and keep warm.

🫕 When the meat has been removed from the pot, add the parsnips, carrots, turnip, onions, and potatoes to the beef stock. Simmer for 15 minutes. Add the cabbage; simmer 15 minutes longer. Return the beef to the pot and reheat.

🫕 To serve, slice the beef very thin and arrange in the center of a large platter. Surround the beef with the vegetables from the pot and the warm beets. Sprinkle with parsley. Serves 8-10.

Serve with horseradish, mustard, and slices of hot corn bread.

Use any leftovers to make Red Flannel Hash (page 18), the name for this dish, which is colored by the beets, suggests the red hue of flannel shirts and winter underwear!

Red Flannel Hash

¼ pound salt pork, diced
1 medium-size onion, chopped
3 cups chopped, cooked potatoes
2 cups chopped, cooked corned beef
1 cup chopped, cooked beets
Salt and pepper to taste
¼ cup heavy cream

In a large skillet, fry the pork until crisp; remove with a slotted spoon and reserve. Add the onion to the skillet and cook until tender; remove to a large bowl. Add the potatoes, beef, beets, salt, pepper, and cream to the onion; mix well. Heat the fat remaining in the skillet. Add the hash mixture; spread and press evenly in the pan. Cook, uncovered, over medium heat until browned and crusty on the bottom, about 35-40 minutes. Place a large, round platter over the skillet and carefully invert the hash onto the platter. Sprinkle with the reserved salt pork. Serves 4.

Excellent served with poached eggs.

Fannie Daddies (Fried Clams)

3 eggs, separated
1 cup milk
2 tablespoons salad oil
2 cups all-purpose flour
½ teaspoon salt
2 tablespoons lemon juice
1 quart shucked clams, well drained
Oil for frying

In a large bowl, beat the egg yolks until thick; beat in the milk, 2 tablespoons oil, flour, salt, and lemon juice. In a separate bowl, beat the egg whites until stiff; fold into the batter. Add the drained clams. Chill the mixture for 2-4 hours. In a deep fryer or heavy saucepan, pour in enough oil to measure 2-3 inches deep. Heat to 375°F. Add the clams, several at a time, and fry until puffed and golden, about 3 minutes. Remove with a slotted spoon and drain well on paper towels. Serves 4-6.

Serve with tartar sauce and thick slices of French bread.

Codfish Cakes

1 pound salt cod
6 medium-size potatoes, peeled and quartered
2 eggs
1 teaspoon Worcestershire sauce
½ teaspoon pepper
1 teaspoon dry mustard
3 tablespoons shortening

- The day before serving, wash the salt cod under running water for 15 minutes. Place in a glass, enamel, or stainless steel pan; cover with cold water. Soak the fish about 24 hours, changing the water 3 or 4 times. Drain; rinse the fish under running water for 5 minutes. Place in a large saucepan; cover with cold water; bring to a boil. Simmer the fish uncovered about 20 minutes. Drain. Remove and discard the skin and bones. Shred the fish into fine flakes with a fork. You should have 2 cups of flaked fish.
- Cook the potatoes in boiling water until tender, about 15 minutes; drain. Place

them in a large bowl and mash to a smooth puree. Beat in the fish, eggs, Worcestershire sauce, pepper, and dry mustard. Shape the mixture into 12 patties. In a large skillet, melt the shortening over medium heat. Fry each patty until browned, about 10 minutes on each side. Serves 6.

Hearty breakfast fare in colonial times — the codfish cakes were served with baked beans and brown bread!

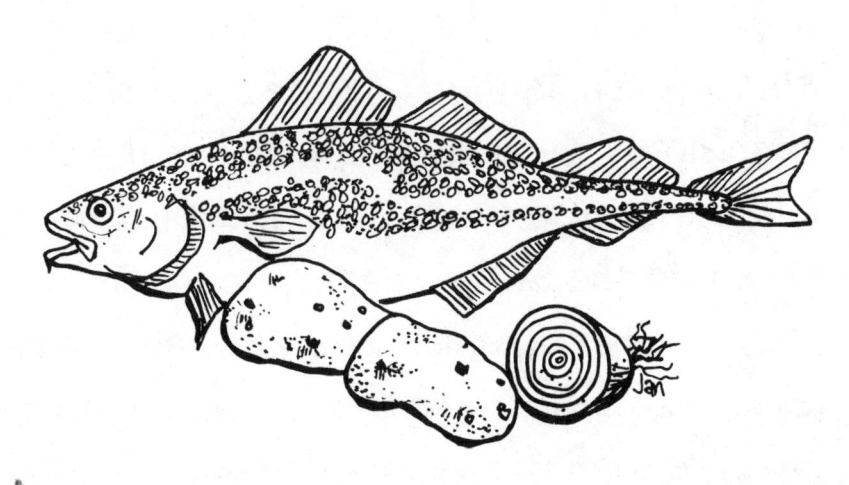

Lobster Newburg

6 tablespoons butter
3 tablespoons all-purpose flour
2 cups light cream
3 egg yolks, beaten
2½ cups cooked, cubed lobster meat
⅓ cup cooking sherry
2 teaspoons lemon juice
½ teaspoon salt
Paprika

In a large skillet or chafing dish, melt the butter over medium heat; blend in the flour. Gradually stir in the cream. Cook slowly, stirring constantly, until the sauce starts to thicken. Stir a small amount of the sauce into the beaten yolks; pour this mixture back into the skillet. Stir in the lobster, cooking sherry, lemon juice, and salt. Continue cooking and stirring until thick; do not boil. Sprinkle with the paprika. Serve immediately. Serves 4-6.

Serve in patty shells, on steamed rice, or over hot, buttered toast points.

Maple Acorn Squash

4 medium-size acorn squashes
$\frac{3}{4}$ cup pure maple syrup
1 teaspoon cinnamon
$\frac{1}{2}$ teaspoon nutmeg
$\frac{1}{4}$ teaspoon cloves
$\frac{1}{2}$ teaspoon salt
$\frac{1}{4}$ cup melted butter
8 ($\frac{1}{2}$-inch) pieces bacon

Cut each squash in half; remove the seeds and fibers. Arrange the halves cut side up in a large shallow baking pan. In a small bowl, blend together the maple syrup, cinnamon, nutmeg, cloves, salt, and melted butter. Spoon about 2 tablespoons of the syrup mixture into the hollow of each squash. Top with a piece of bacon. Add boiling water to the pan to measure about 1 inch deep. Bake in a preheated 350°F oven until tender, about 1 hour. Serves 8.

A Christmas favorite.

Baked Beans

2 pounds dried white beans
   (great northern, navy, or pea beans)
½ cup pure maple syrup
½ cup brown sugar, packed
½ teaspoon salt
½ teaspoon pepper
1 medium-size apple, peeled and chopped
1 large onion, diced
¼ pound salt pork, scored

In a large saucepan, cover the beans with cold water and soak overnight. Drain; cover with fresh cold water. Simmer for 30 minutes or until the bean skins roll back when you blow on them. Drain, reserving the cooking liquid. Add the maple syrup, brown sugar, salt, and pepper to the liquid. Put the beans in a large bean pot. Stir in the apple and onion. Pour the reserved cooking liquid over the bean mixture to cover. (Reserve any remaining liquid.) Sink the salt pork into the center. Bake in a 275°F oven for

4 hours or until tender. Stir every 30 minutes to release the starches and thicken the liquid. Add the reserved bean liquid to keep the beans covered. Serves 10-12.

The long, slow cooking which allows the flavors to mingle is the secret ingredient in this traditional New England dish.

Corn Pudding

2 eggs
1½ cups milk
1½ teaspoons sugar
¼ teaspoon salt
⅛ teaspoon pepper
2 cups whole kernel corn (fresh or canned, drained)
¾ cup cracker crumbs
2 tablespoons butter or margarine

In a large bowl, combine the eggs, milk, sugar, salt, and pepper; beat well with a wire whisk. Stir in the corn. Pour into a well-greased 1½-quart casserole. Mix together the cracker crumbs and butter or margarine until crumbly. Sprinkle over the top of the corn mixture. Bake in a preheated 350°F oven until a knife inserted near the center comes out clean, about 1 hour. Serves 4-6.

Variations: Add ½ cup grated cheese and ¼ cup chopped green pepper. Add 1 (7½-ounce) can minced clams, well drained.

Cranberry-Nut Muffins

2 3/4 cups all-purpose flour
3/4 cup sugar
4 teaspoons baking powder
1/2 teaspoon salt
1 cup milk
1 egg, slightly beaten
1/4 cup shortening, melted
1 cup coarsely chopped cranberries
1/2 cup chopped walnuts
1 tablespoon grated orange peel

Combine the flour, sugar, baking powder, and salt. In a separate bowl, mix together the milk, egg, and shortening; add to the flour mixture. Stir until just moist. Stir in the chopped cranberries, nuts, and orange peel. Fill greased muffin cups about two-thirds full. Bake in a preheated 400°F oven for 20-25 minutes. Remove the muffins from the pan and cool on a wire rack. Makes 12 muffins.

Serve warm with whipped cream cheese.

Anadama Bread

½ cup yellow cornmeal
3 tablespoons butter or margarine
¼ cup unsulphured molasses
1 teaspoon salt
¾ cup boiling water
1 package active dry yeast
¼ cup warm water
2½ cups all-purpose flour

Combine the cornmeal, butter or margarine, molasses, and salt in a large bowl. Stir in the boiling water and let stand until lukewarm. Dissolve the yeast in the ¼ cup warm water. Add the dissolved yeast and 1¼ cups of the flour to the cornmeal mixture; beat until smooth. Gradually beat in the remaining 1¼ cups flour to make a smooth dough. Cover the bowl with a towel; let rise in a warm place until the dough is doubled in bulk, about 1 hour. Punch down; shape into a round loaf. Place in a greased 2-quart round casserole. Cover; let rise in a warm place until doubled, about 45 minutes. Bake in a preheated 350°F oven until the loaf sounds hollow when tapped, about 35 minutes. Remove the bread from the casserole and cool on a wire rack. Serve warm or toasted. Makes 1 round loaf.

According to legend, this bread was invented by a fisherman from Gloucester, Massachusetts, who had a lazy wife named Anna. Anna refused to bake bread. So one evening, the fisherman added yeast, molasses, and flour to his usual cornmeal mush supper and baked it himself, all the while muttering, "Anna, damn her!"

Try this bread toasted with apple butter for breakfast.

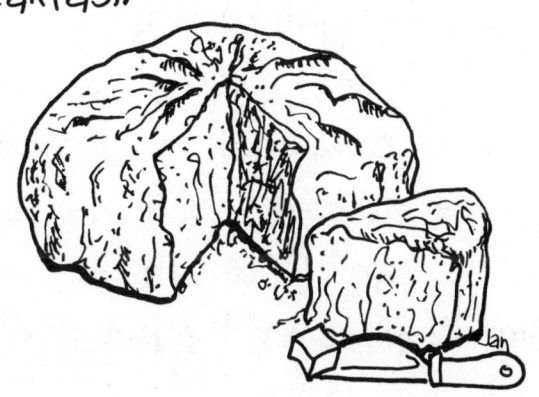

Brown Bread

1 cup all-purpose flour
1 cup yellow cornmeal
1 cup whole wheat flour
2 teaspoons baking soda
1 teaspoon salt
¾ cup unsulphured molasses
2 cups buttermilk or sour milk
¾ cup raisins

In a large bowl, combine the all-purpose flour, cornmeal, whole wheat flour, baking soda, and salt. In a separate bowl, beat together the molasses and buttermilk or sour milk; stir in the raisins. Add the molasses mixture to the dry ingredients and mix well. Fill 2 well-greased 1-pound coffee cans about three-fourths full. Cover each can tightly with a circle of buttered aluminum foil; tie in place with kitchen string. Set the cans on a rack in a large pot. Pour in boiling water to come about halfway up the sides of the cans. Return the water to a boil over high heat; cover the pot tightly and reduce the heat to low. Steam the bread for about 2½ hours or until a wooden pick inserted in the center of each loaf comes out clean. Immediately remove the bread from the cans; cool on a wire rack. Makes 2 loaves.

Serve warm, thick slices with baked beans and codfish cakes.

Johnnycakes

1 cup white cornmeal
½ teaspoon salt
1 cup boiling water
⅓-½ cup milk

Place the cornmeal and salt in a large bowl; stir in the boiling water. Mix well and let stand for 10 minutes. Beat in enough milk to make a batter stiff enough to hold its shape on a spoon. Drop the batter by the tablespoon into a lightly greased skillet. Cook over medium heat until golden and crisp around the edges, about 3 minutes on each side. Serve immediately. Makes about 12.

Serve warm with butter or with butter and maple syrup.

The name evolved from "journeycake," because these thin cornmeal pancakes were often carried for sustenance on long trips.

Maine Blueberry Pie

Pastry for a 9-inch double-crust pie
½ cup sugar
¼ cup all-purpose flour
1 tablespoon lemon juice
4 cups fresh blueberries
2 tablespoons butter or margarine
1 egg white, slightly beaten (optional)

Roll out half the dough to form a bottom crust and place in a 9-inch pie pan. Mix together the sugar, flour, and lemon juice. Sprinkle over the berries; let stand for 10 minutes. Turn the berries into the pie shell; dot with the butter or margarine. Roll out the remaining pastry; place on top of the berries; press the edges together; trim. Flute the edges; cut slits in the top. Brush with the egg white. Bake in a preheated 400°F oven for 30-35 minutes. Remove to a wire rack; cool. Serves 6-8.

Best served warm with rich vanilla ice cream

Boston Cream Pie

Cake:
- ⅓ cup butter or margarine
- ¾ cup sugar
- 1 egg
- 2 cups all-purpose flour
- 2½ teaspoons baking powder
- ½ teaspoon salt
- 1 cup milk
- 1 teaspoon vanilla extract

In a large bowl, cream together the butter or margarine and sugar; add the egg and mix well. In a separate bowl, combine the flour, baking powder, and salt. Add to the butter mixture alternately with the milk, beating well after each addition. Stir in the vanilla. Pour into 2 greased 9-inch cake pans. Bake in a preheated 350°F oven for 20-25 minutes. Remove to wire racks; cool for 10 minutes. Remove the cake from the pans; cool completely.

Filling:
- ½ cup sugar
- 3 tablespoons cornstarch

1 cup milk, scalded
2 eggs, slightly beaten
1 tablespoon butter or margarine
1 teaspoon vanilla extract

Combine the sugar and cornstarch in a large saucepan; gradually stir in the milk. Cook slowly over medium heat, stirring frequently, until the mixture thickens, 10-15 minutes. Stir a small amount of the hot sauce into the eggs; pour this mixture back into the saucepan. Continue cooking and stirring until the sauce becomes very thick, about 3 more minutes. Remove from the heat; stir in the butter or margarine and vanilla.

Icing:
2 squares unsweetened chocolate
2 tablespoons butter or margarine
$\frac{1}{2}$ teaspoon vanilla extract
2 cups confectioners' sugar
$\frac{1}{4}$ cup hot water

In a medium-size saucepan, melt the chocolate over low heat; stir in the butter or margarine and vanilla. Remove from the heat; add the confectioners' sugar alternately with the hot water; beat until smooth. Add more water if a thinner glaze is desired.

🍯 To assemble the pie, place one cake layer on a serving dish. Spread with the custard filling; cover with the second cake layer. Leaving the sides exposed, frost the top with the chocolate icing.

Not really a pie, this is a custard-filled cake.

Maple Pumpkin Pie

Crust: ½ cup margarine or butter
⅓ cup brown sugar, packed
1¼ cups all-purpose flour
½ cup chopped nuts
¼ teaspoon baking soda
½ teaspoon vanilla extract

Mix together the margarine or butter and brown sugar in a large bowl. Stir in the remaining ingredients until crumbly. Press the mixture onto the bottom and sides of a 9-inch pie pan, building up a ½-inch edge. Set aside.

Filling: 2 eggs
½ cup brown sugar, packed
½ cup maple syrup
½ teaspoon cinnamon
½ teaspoon ginger
½ teaspoon nutmeg
2 cups pumpkin puree
1 cup light cream

Combine all the filling ingredients in a large bowl; beat until smooth. Pour into the prepared crust. Cover the edges of the crust with foil to prevent excessive browning. Bake in a preheated 375°F oven for 55-60 minutes or until a knife inserted near the center comes out clean. Cool on a wire rack. Serves 6-8.

Substitute a 9-inch unbaked pie shell for the fancy cookie crust if desired.

Top with a dollop of fresh whipped cream.

Indian Pudding

3 cups milk
1/4 cup yellow cornmeal
2 tablespoons butter or margarine
1/4 cup unsulphured molasses
1 egg, slightly beaten
1/4 cup sugar
1/2 teaspoon salt
1/2 teaspoon ginger
1 teaspoon cinnamon

In a large saucepan, scald the milk. Using a wire whisk, gradually stir in the cornmeal. Cook over medium heat, stirring occasionally, until the mixture thickens and coats a metal spoon, about 10 minutes. Stir in the butter or margarine; remove from the heat. In a separate bowl, combine the molasses, egg, sugar, salt, ginger, and cinnamon. Gradually stir into the milk mixture. Pour into a greased 1½-quart casserole. Bake in a preheated 325°F oven until a knife inserted near the center comes out clean, about 1 hour. Serve warm. Serves 4.

Joe Froggers (Soft Molasses Cookies)

¾ cup shortening
¾ cup sugar
1 cup unsulphured molasses
4½ cups all-purpose flour
3 teaspoons baking powder
½ teaspoon salt
1 teaspoon baking soda
2 teaspoons ginger
⅔ cup water

In a large bowl, cream together the shortening and sugar; blend in the molasses. In a separate bowl, combine the flour, baking powder, salt, baking soda, and ginger. Add alternately with the water to the molasses mixture; mix well. Form the dough into a ball; cover with plastic wrap and chill for at least 1 hour. On a lightly floured surface, roll out the dough, half at a time, to ¼-inch thickness. Cut into 4-inch rounds with a floured cutter. Place the cookies on greased baking sheets. Bake in a preheated 350°F oven until lightly browned, about

10 minutes. Remove the cookies to wire racks; cool. Makes 24 large cookies.

These cookies were named for Uncle Joe, an elderly black man who lived by a frog pond in Marblehead, Massachusetts. He used to trade the cookies for rum from the local fishermen.

Maple Cutouts

1 cup butter or margarine
1/3 cup sugar
1/2 cup pure maple syrup
1/3 cup milk
3 1/2 cups all-purpose flour
1/2 teaspoon baking soda
1/2 teaspoon ginger
* Maple glaze

In a medium-size saucepan, combine the butter or margarine, sugar, and maple syrup; bring to a boil. Remove from the heat; cool. Stir in the milk. In a large bowl, combine the flour, baking soda, and ginger. Stir in the cooled syrup mixture; mix well. Form the dough into a ball; cover with plastic wrap and chill for at least 1 hour. On a lightly floured surface, roll out the dough, half at a time, to 1/4-inch thickness. Cut into shapes with floured cookie cutters. Place on ungreased baking sheets. Bake in a preheated 375°F oven for 8-10 minutes. Remove the cookies to wire racks; cool. Spread with the glaze. Makes about 36 cookies.

*<u>Maple glaze</u>: In a small bowl, blend ½ cup confectioners' sugar with 3 tablespoons pure maple syrup.

Cranberry Apple Crisp

2 cups coarsely chopped cranberries
6-8 medium-size apples, peeled and sliced
¾ cup white sugar
½ cup butter or margarine
1 cup rolled oats
½ cup all-purpose flour
½ cup brown sugar
½ teaspoon nutmeg

Combine the cranberries, apples, and white sugar in a greased 1½-quart casserole. Melt the butter or margarine in a medium-size saucepan. Stir in the oats, flour, brown sugar, and nutmeg; mix well. Spread over the apples and berries. Bake in a preheated 350°F oven for 1 hour. Serve warm. Serves 6.

This tart-sweet dessert is best topped with ice cream.

Blueberry Grunt

Dumplings: 2 cups all-purpose flour
  1 tablespoon sugar
  2 teaspoons baking powder
  1 egg
  ½ cup milk

Combine the flour, sugar, and baking powder. In a separate bowl, beat the egg with the milk; add to the flour mixture. Stir until just moist.

Fruit: 2 cups water
  ½ cup sugar
  ¼ teaspoon nutmeg
  1 tablespoon lemon juice
  4 cups blueberries

Combine all of the filling ingredients in a large skillet. Bring to a rolling boil; reduce the heat. Drop the dumplings by the tablespoon onto the simmering berries, leaving space between dumplings. Cover the skillet and simmer for 20 minutes. To serve, spoon the warm blueberry sauce over the dumplings in individual bowls. Serves 6.

No-Cook Cranberry Relish

- 2 large thin-skinned oranges
- 2 large apples
- 1 pound (4 cups) fresh cranberries
- 1½ cups sugar

Cut the oranges and apples into quarters; remove any seeds. Using a food processor, process the oranges, apples, and cranberries until coarsely chopped. Transfer to a large serving bowl. Add the sugar; mix well. (Adjust the sugar to taste.) Cover the bowl with plastic wrap and let stand at room temperature for 24 hours before serving. Tightly covered, the relish can be stored for up to 3 weeks in the refrigerator. Makes about 5 cups.

A New England favorite to serve with poultry or pork.

Mincemeat

2 pounds chopped lean beef
1 pound chopped beef suet
12 cups chopped apples (about 4 pounds)
2 pounds raisins
2 pounds currants
½ pound chopped candied citron
Juice and chopped rind of 2 oranges
Juice and chopped rind of 2 lemons
1 cup honey
1 cup unsulphured molasses
1 tablespoon cinnamon
1 tablespoon allspice
2 teaspoons nutmeg
1 teaspoon cloves
1 teaspoon ginger
3 cups cider
1 cup brandy (optional)
2 cups coarsely chopped nuts (optional)

Combine all of the ingredients in a large pot. Simmer over low heat for about 2 hours, stirring frequently. To freeze:

Package cooled mincemeat in clean freezer containers; seal and freeze. To can: Ladle the hot mincemeat into hot, sterilized canning jars, leaving 1-inch headspace. Adjust lids. Process pints and quarts in a boiling water bath for 90 minutes. Makes about 6 quarts.

Mincemeat is best prepared several weeks before using.

Use 4 cups homemade mincemeat for one 9-inch double-crust pie.

For a spicy twist on tradition, substitute 1 cup of mincemeat for 1 of the 2 cups of pumpkin when baking the Maple Pumpkin Pie on page 37.

Hot Clam Appetizers

1 (7½-ounce) can minced clams, drained
½ cup mayonnaise
½ cup grated Parmesan cheese
1 tablespoon finely chopped onion
1 tablespoon finely chopped green pepper
1 tablespoon Worcestershire sauce
Melba or rye toast rounds
Paprika

Combine the clams, mayonnaise, cheese, onion, green pepper, and Worcestershire sauce; mix well. Heap the mixture onto the toast rounds; sprinkle with paprika. Place the rounds on baking sheets and broil 4 inches below the heat source until lightly toasted and heated through. Serve warm. Makes about 36 appetizers.

These easy but elegant appetizers can be prepared ahead, refrigerated, and broiled in the oven just before serving.